BUBBA AND BUDDHA

walk into the sushi bar

7 SECRETS *of* MINDFUL CUSTOMER SERVICE AND BUSINESS SUCCESS

PAM BENSON

First published by Dog Ear Publishing
4010 W. 86th Street, Ste H
Indianapolis, IN 46268
www.dogearpublishing.net

ISBN: 978-1-4575-2653-4

This book is printed on acid-free paper.

Printed in the United States of America

Only a life lived in the service
to others is worth living.

~ Albert Einstein, Nobel laureate physicist

TABLE OF CONTENTS

INTRODUCTION

Robert Dedman was long known as the richest man in golf, and with good reason. His company, ClubCorp, developed country clubs and city clubs, as well as golf resorts, all across the United States, beginning with Brookhaven Country Club in Dallas, Texas, and expanding to include purchases of Pinehurst, Barton Creek, and the Homestead, among others. Dedman is one of my heroes, not just because he was a fellow Texan but also because he understood that the key to success wasn't just the quality of his golf courses or the size of the drinks and burgers in the clubhouses—it was the quality of *personal service* provided to each and every customer. Dedman, known for his folksy wisdom, used to say, "If you serve the classes, you'll eat with the masses, but if you serve the masses, you'll eat with the classes." In other words, if you cater only to rich people, you'll never be one of them, but if you cater to a broad mass market, treating each and every customer as if they were upper class, you'll become rich. By making a lot of people happy, you'll make a lot of money.

I've spent my entire life in the service business, coming from a family of restaurateurs. I grew up working in my dad's restaurants and knew that this was the life for me. I went to college and earned my degree in English, but it didn't change my career goals. Serving others brings me joy. To me, serving others in a warm, inviting environment with wonderful food is the best thing in the world!

When I was just twenty-five years old, I bought a Victorian house in the hospital district of Ft. Worth and opened my first restaurant, Ms Tilly's. In no time at all, we became known for our delicious home-baked Ms Tilly's Apple Pie. We knew we had a hit on our hands when we sold more than a thousand apple pies—by the slice—at the annual Mayfest. Now that's a lot of slices!

My next venture was the Jubilee Café, in Ft. Worth's Cultural district, where we were famous for our down-home cooking. I

am especially proud of the fact that it was a real gathering place where everyone from the community came together to break bread and share a meal. Everyone from judges and politicians to local business people to families with kids to young couples out on a date came to enjoy warm, homey dining experiences under one roof. We won many awards for our chicken-fried steak, a classic favorite among Southerners.

With the success of the Jubilee Café, our chicken-fried steak earned us enough acclaim for me to be invited to participate in Ft. Worth's Sister City Program. I traveled to Nagaoka, Japan, with thirty other people from Ft. Worth, including the mayor, for a cultural exchange of music, art, and food. We held a cooking school in a hotel in Nagaoka, where we introduced the Japanese to chicken-fried steak and another Southern classic, pecan pie. Both were huge hits!

Over the years, many new restaurateurs have asked my advice as they worked to establish their own brand in a very competitive business. Other entrepreneurs sometimes ask my advice as well, so I decided to distill some of the key lessons I've learned over the years—along with a few additional tips from my fellow customer-service experts—and write them down to share them more easily. The slender volume you hold in your hands is the result. We're not talking War and Peace here. Delivering distinctive customer service to build a successful business is not complicated—it's simple—but keep in mind that it's simple but not easy. It takes commitment, consistency, continuous improvement, and creativity, as well as character, compassion, and courage.

If you're interested in learning what it takes to run a productive and profitable business, this book is for you. Read it and reap great results!

Pam Benson

CULTIVATE BEGINNER'S MIND

If your mind is empty, it is always ready for anything; it is open to everything. In the beginner's mind there are many possibilities; in the expert's mind there are few.

~ Shunryu Suzuki, Japanese Zen priest, author of *Zen Mind, Beginner's Mind*

THE ZEN MASTER
AND THE PROFESSOR

Nan-in, a Japanese master during the Meiji era (1868–1912), received a university professor who came to inquire about Zen.

Nan-in served tea. He poured his visitor's cup full … and then kept on pouring.

The professor watched the overflow until he no longer could restrain himself. "It is overfull. No more will go in!" he exclaimed.

"Like this cup," Nan-in said, "you are full of your own opinions and speculations. How can I show you Zen unless you first empty your cup?"

BEGINNER'S MIND

1

Who among us doesn't take pride in being smart and knowledgeable? Don't we like to think we know a lot about many things, especially customer service? After all, we have been customers ourselves, thousands of times, in a wide variety of situations, dealing with many different products and services. It's safe to say that many of us think we're experts on the topic of customer service.

But if that is true, why do so many people complain about the service they receive from airlines, department stores, restaurants, local mom-and-pop stores, boutiques, car dealerships, fast-food establishments, dry cleaners, grocery stores, auto repair shops, coffeeshops, and myriad other places of business?

If everyone already knows how to deliver great customer service and is delivering it, why do we have online rating services like Yelp? We would have no need for the Better Business Bureau or J.D. Power or Zagat or Consumer Reports if all business owners and service employees were as smart about customer service as they think they are.

The truth is, it is precisely our attitude—"Of course I know what good customer service is"—that too often gets in the way of delivering that very service, because when we think we're experts, we close our minds to learning. When we think we know it all, we close our eyes and ears to new information. When we're sure we already *know* what our customers want, we are blind and deaf to what they *really* want.

Cultivating beginner's mind means not making assumptions. It means approaching each new customer with an open mind and an open heart. Having beginner's mind means being curious: *Who is this customer? I wonder what's important to this customer. I'm eager to know how I can help. Let's find how who this customer is and what his/her needs are.*

Beginner's mind isn't just for dealing with customers; it's a posture we adopt toward everyone and everything: interacting with coworkers, confronting an unexpected problem, handling

mistakes, working with our bosses, learning new skills, taking on new jobs (or new duties within an old job), facing any and all situations, familiar or unfamiliar. Beginner's mind is a way of living and working all day, every day.

Above all, cultivating beginner's mind means being fully available in the present moment, not thinking about something that happened in the past, and not worrying about something that might happen in the future. Mindful customer service means being fully awake, fully present, living in the moment—*this* moment.

Beginners mind means learning how to LISTEN.

Lean in to establish rapport.

Interpret feelings as well as words.

Stay connected through eye contact.

Tune in to what's not being said as well as what is.

Express empathy and understanding.

Never interrupt, criticize, or judge …
just LISTEN.

1

Suzuki Roshi once said, "The essence of Zen is 'Not Always So.'" "Not always so." It's a good little phrase to carry around when you're sure. It gives you an opportunity to look again more carefully and see what other possibilities there might be in the situation.

~ Abbess Zenkei Blanche Hartman

Minds are like parachutes – they only function when open.

~ Lord Thomas Dewar, Scottish businessman

SELLING CARS TO DIVERSE CUSTOMERS

by BJ Gallagher

Years ago, early in my career as a workshop leader and trainer, I used to teach customer-service classes at car dealerships in California. The focus was on customer diversity and on teaching car salespeople, service writers, and parts department folks how to serve the needs of diverse customers. California has more ethnic and cultural diversity than most other states, and dealerships were concerned that they were losing sales because of inadvertent stereotyping and/or cultural insensitivity on the part of their employees. They were right to be concerned—they *were indeed* losing sales!

Their number-one problem: Dealership employees thought they were experts in sizing up prospective buyers. They prided themselves on being able to tell a serious buyer from a mere looky-loo. They thought they could tell who had money and who didn't. They made snap judgments about the people who came onto their car lots. They would take one look at what kind of car the person had driven up in; what the person's license plate rim said; what gender, age and ethnicity the customer was; how the customer was dressed; and who the real decision maker was if customers came in couples or families. Sales guys didn't want to waste their time on someone who wasn't going to buy a car that day, because they worked on a commission-only basis, so they did their best to get very good at sizing people up quickly, within mere seconds.

This type of attitude—"I'm good at sizing people up"—is the very antithesis of beginner's mind. Thinking you know who people really are by simply taking a quick look at their physical appearance is arrogance—and ignorance—of the highest form. It is the arrogance of the "expert"—the one who thinks he knows it all.

1

What was most surprising was that just about every salesperson could tell me about a time when his judgment had been just flat wrong and he had lost a sale because of it. One salesman in Santa Barbara told me how a customer dressed like a lumberjack had come into the dealership one day, unshaven and dirty, wearing a plaid flannel shirt, scruffy jeans, and beat-up old boots. He was interested in looking at Jeeps. The salesman blew him off and turned him over to a young guy who was new at the dealership. An hour later, the sale was made—all cash—and the lumberjack guy drove off in a brand-new Jeep Grand Cherokee with all the bells and whistles. When the experienced sales guy asked the junior guy about the sale, the newbie said, "Oh, didn't you recognize him? That was Kenny Loggins, the singer. He has a ranch near here." The old guy was still kicking himself years later for having misjudged this wealthy customer.

Another salesman at a Southern California Acura dealership told me how a young teenager came onto the lot one day, asking to see the latest cool new Acura sports coupe. The kid wasn't even sixteen yet, so the salesman knew he couldn't drive. "The car over there on the showroom floor, kid. Surrounded by velvet ropes. You can look, but don't touch it." Then he turned and walked away. A little later that afternoon, the kid bought the car. When the salesman heard that one of the new young saleswomen at the dealership had made the sale, he confronted her. "How the heck did that kid buy a car?" he demanded. She smiled at him and answered, "He bought the car for his dad for Father's Day. The kid is a child actor—he paid cash."

I could go on and on, giving you hundreds of examples of how automotive professionals offend their customers and lose sales by prequalifying the very people they're supposed to be selling to. These car guys are not bad people; they're just under the illusion that you can size people up within just a few seconds. They consider themselves experts, which is the opposite of having a beginner's mind. They think they know it all, when in reality, they know nothing.

Remember that old saying, "You can't judge a book by its cover." It's true—not just of books, but of people, too. It's espe-

cially true of people. And we are all guilty of the same thing that these car guys were guilty of: making assumptions about customers based only on their appearance. The truth is, you and I are no different from the car guys; we do it, too. We make assumptions about people all the time, based on very little real information. The only difference between you and me and the car guys is that we probably make most of our assumptions quietly, in our own heads, while the car guys brag about their ability to evaluate people. We all do it; they're just more open about the fact that they do it.

Why are we so quick to judge others, especially those we've just met? Is it because we're bad people? Are we sexist, racist, ageist, or any other form of bigot? No. It's simply because the human mind thinks in categories and because the senses take in impressions and perceptions at rapid-fire speed all day long, and the mind works at lightning speed to organize all that incoming data. It's as if your mind looks like a wall of cubbyholes, with a label on each. As your eyes, ears, nose, and other senses take in data, your mind stashes it away as simply and as quickly as it can, so you can function and interact with the world around you.

The problem is, our brains usually don't stop to question the data as they come in. The mind doesn't say, "That guy looks like a street bum … hmmm, I wonder, is that who he truly is?" Nope, the mind just organizes and categorizes the data. Then we proceed as if the mind has categorized correctly.

If we are to cultivate beginner's mind, we must continually question our minds. We must challenge what we think we know, based on what we perceive. We must train ourselves to look beyond first impressions. We must question what we think we're seeing. We must approach every person—and every situation—in the spirit of an explorer, a student, an adventurer who wants to know the truth behind the illusion of superficial appearances.

Beginner's mind requires humility—an open mind—and a desire to learn and grow.

If we are not customer-driven,
our cars won't be either.

~ Donald Peterson, former CEO, Ford Motor Company

TIPS AND TOOLS:

Here are a few tips for cultivating beginner's bind.

Focus on one thing at a time. So often, our attention is distracted and diminished by dwelling in the past or worrying about the future. We can easily get overwhelmed by projecting what-ifs into the future and trying to figure out how we can prevent bad things from happening. Or we wallow in remorse and regret over things that have already happened, as if replaying them in our minds could change things. Cultivating beginner's mind means letting go of the past, ignoring the future, and focusing on what's right in front of you. Just take the next apparent step.

Let go of old habits. If you drove to work along the same route day after day, year after year, your world would be very small and you wouldn't see much that was new and interesting. You wouldn't grow and learn every day. Try letting go of your habitual way of getting to work, and see what happens. Try letting go of your habitual ways of doing other things, and see how your world expands.

Be willing to set aside what you think you already know. Approach each person, each task, each situation as if you know nothing. Be curious. Ask questions. Discover things you would never find out as an expert. Let go of any and all assumptions.

Let go of ego and practice humility instead. Your ego is a hindrance to serving others. It's also a hindrance to learning, growing, and exploring new possibilities. If you need to impress others, you'll never be teachable. Try this: Instead of feeling like you have to have all the answers, practice asking good questions. Beginners are experts at asking good questions; beginners are experts at growing and learning.

Remember, Zen master Shunryu Suzuki said, "In the mind of the beginner there are many possibilities." If you allow yourself to start over—whether it's learning a skill or establishing a relationship with a new customer—you'll discover new possibilities and a new freedom.

ATTITUDE REALLY *IS* EVERYTHING

If you work just for money, you'll never make it, but if you love what you're doing and you always put the customer first, success will be yours.

~ Ray Kroc, founder of McDonald's

YOUR ATTITUDE IS WHAT ANIMATES YOU

by Chip R. Bell

I knew I had a treat in the offing when the answer to my where's-the-best-lunch-in-town question got escalated to "White's is the best in the state!" I was almost out of earshot when the local on the street corner added, "Ask for Katie."

The target of the local's affinity was White's Restaurant in Salem, Oregon. The restaurant had the look of a 1935 diner. The inside was neat and spotless, the atmosphere warm and upbeat. The hostess on the other side of the "please wait to be seated" sign gave us a bright Steinway smile as I crossed the threshold.

"I heard Katie was the best in the house," I announced. "I'd like her table."

"Well, well, well . . . it's your lucky day!" the hostess teased. "There's is normally a two-hour wait to get Katie, but we just had a cancellation," she said with a wink and a grin. "I think I can squeeze you in." The needle on my fun meter was already racing to the top.

"We are so glad to have you!" said our waitress. Her words came straight from the frying pan of a zealous spirit. "I'm Katie, and I'll check back with you in a minute. You know it's Thursday. Don's vegetable soup is already getting rave reviews." I was beginning to feel like a local.

When I noticed that the breakfast menu listed Don's Big Mess as a headliner and that the burger choices included a Whoopee! Burger, I began to think I'd walked into a comedy club. My spirit registered another uptick.

People throughout the restaurant were engaged in warm conversation, noisily greeting people they knew as they came through the front door. An hour later, I was back outside with a satisfied stomach and a very happy heart. The meal was awesome, but it was the animated service that had told me I was witnessing the spirit of "take their breath away."

"Animation" is a moniker for the clear and present energy that reflects an unmistakable joy of serving. The label reminds me of what a great cartoonist does in turning stills into moving pictures—like the late Chuck Jones, who created such famous cartoon characters as Bugs Bunny, Daffy Duck, Wile E. Coyote, Road Runner, and Pepe Le Pew. When I interviewed him a few years back, the then eighty-eight-year-old genius sat in his studio in Irvine, California, and reflected on his sixty-plus years as a world-renowned animator. "The secret to making a character come alive," he mused, "is not how you draw that particular character. Animation happens when everything in the frame moves with the character."

The power of animated service people is how those people help everything around them move with them. Katie was an animator. But then, so was everything about the restaurant in which she worked.

What's behind the sparkly Katie I witnessed at White's? What fuels her nonstop "spirit of greatness"? Katie selected the attitude she knew would likely unveil a customer smile and help boomerang that same spirit back. Her attitude is what philosopher/psychologist Rollo May had in mind when he wrote, "There is an energy field between all humans. When we reach out in passion it is met with an answering passion."

Consider the characters that kids the world over enjoy seeing at Disney theme parks. How can Mickey be Mickey, no matter what the circumstances? There is no "Mickey shot" to inoculate the character against crying babies, surly guests, or a costume without air-conditioning. Mickey (like all the characters) selects the Mickey attitude to exhibit "on stage" without regard to whether it is Monday morning or the day after late-night TV. It is the cast member in the Mickey costume who selects the Mickey attitude.

Eighty-five percent of success in life, according to a well-known and frequently cited Harvard study, is due solely to attitude. An attitude that shows the spirit of greatness provides the

energy and magnetism needed to deliver an animated experience for customers and to draw devotion from them. Although
customers like dealing with employees who are committed,
they absolutely love being served by someone whose spirit to
serve is unmistakable in its passion, pride, and commitment.
Occasional animation is not sufficient. It is both the consistency and sincerity of attitude that brings customers back and
causes them to tell all of their friends to "ask for Katie."

Attitude can take the plain vanilla out of almost any
encounter. German philosopher Johann von Goethe called it
"boldness" and said, "Whatever you can do, or dream you can,
begin in boldness. Boldness has genius, power, and magic in it.
Until one is committed, there is hesitancy, the chance to draw
back, always ineffectiveness. The moment one definitely com-
mits oneself, then Providence moves, too. All sorts of things
occur to help one that would never otherwise have occurred."
German philosopher Georg Hegel echoed the same theme:
"Nothing great in the world has been accomplished without
passion." Customers may be influenced by reason, but they are
inspired by passion.

The most important thing to know about attitude is that it is
something one *selects*. No normal person comes into the world
with a particular attitude; it is chosen (or not). Although we
could blame our parents, our backgrounds, or our circumstances, the truth is that we choose whether to be heroes or
victims. Eleanor Roosevelt said, "No one can make you feel
inferior without your consent." Unless you are sick or hurt,
your attitude is what you want it to be. Psychologist and con-
centration camp inmate Viktor Frankl observed that the major
reason those who survived did was the fact that they never
saw themselves as victims. "Every thing can be taken from a
man but one thing: the last of the human freedoms—to choose
one's attitude in any given set of circumstances," wrote Frankl
in his classic book *Man's Search for Meaning*.

The second important thing to know is that an animated attitude can be contagious. When we are around happy, upbeat
people, it is much easier for us to join in the spirit—especially
if the invitation to join is coming from someone who clearly
prefers that we enroll. An unbridled spirit has a magnetic

power on customers. It draws out their higher selves. Being in the presence of a Katie causes customers to feel good about themselves. It's difficult to misbehave or stay cranky in their company. Few among us want to drag storm clouds into the perpetually sunny skies of such vivacious life-forms.

University of Rhode Island students enjoy going to the CVS nearby in the Kingston Emporium to buy a snack and to see "the Excellence Lady." The attraction is CVS head cashier Helen "Nonni" Plummer, who bids farewell to every customer with the phrase, "Have an excellent!" Should someone inquire "excellent what?" she quickly adds, "Whatever you want it to be." Her infectious spirit has spread to a Facebook group titled "You Have an Excellent" with hundreds of members.

It is the attitude of those who serve customers that provides customers with a peephole into the values and qualities most revered by the unit or organization. Remember what Chuck Jones said: "Animation happens when everything in the frame moves with the character"? One of the reasons I have such fond memories of White's is the way Katie was a character in the theatrical performance of White's. Katie no doubt helped others get in the spirit of greatness; others, like the wise-cracking hostess, played their roles alongside Katie. And owner Don Uselman—and inventor of the Whoopee! Burger and Don's Big Mess—was the cheerleader for them all.

Think back about your very best friend as child. This was the person who could tease you in a way no one else could get away with. This was the person who could make you laugh, could keep a secret, and could cheer you up when you were feeling downhearted. You had a relationship filled with consistent enthusiasm. It was without pretense, free of anxiety, and laced with consideration and comfort.

As an animated service tactic, *comfort* comes from familiarity. It is all the ways a service-providing organization creates an "I know you" experience. Starbucks gets great marks from customers for turning the order-taking incident into a memory-making relationship. Step up to the counter to place your order, and you'll hear "Tall Skinny Cinnamon Dolce for Chip" repeated several times—the information echoed from customer to clerk to the drink maker (barista) and back to the customer.

The repetition not only creates the security of familiarity; it also enables Starbucks personnel to quickly learn your specific drink preference so you do not have to start at the beginning each time you show up.

Comfort is the product of an emotional connection that feels familiar plus an experience that is anxiety-free. Don always makes Maynard's meatloaf on Wednesday at White's. The turkey club sandwich always tastes so fresh, you expect to see turkey feathers out of the back. Katie always teases her customers. The consistency makes customers feel empowered and secure. The reliability breeds a sense of contentment, the type that says to the customer's dissonance meter, "Calm down; we've been here before, and it's okay."

Katie was more than friendly. She was a pro working with a resourceful team in a well-oiled system. She had the White's menus in my hand before my bottom touched the chair. My wait was not even noticeable. She refilled my iced tea glass without prompting, brought more rolls, and left the check with the caveat "Don't think I'm trying to rush you out. I just don't want you having to look for me when you're ready to leave."

Want to add comfort to your service experience? Take a close look at all the aspects of the experience that could make your customers feel apprehensive or nervous. Take an empathy walk with frequent customers willing to take the time to talk you through every step of their service journeys with the goal of informing you of all the points whern they experience the slightest unease. Call your own unit or organization, disguise your voice, and asked for something out of the ordinary, even something weird. Had I waited a long time for my menu at White's, I might have generalized that delay to the whole dining experience and concluded that lunch was going to take way too long. Had Katie been too hasty to take my order, I might have worried about her accuracy and wondered whether the apple pie I ordered was going to be Marionberry pie instead.

Katie's version of animation works for Katie because she is authentically animated, delivering it in her own Katie fashion. Customers have a well-honed sincerity sonar and will pick up even a hint of hypocrisy. Animation must come from the heart and be filtered through a conspicuous respect for the customer; otherwise, it will feel as phony as a politician at a barbeque shaking hands and kissing babies. When you are Mickey Mouse, the costume can disguise your true self, but when you are serving "out of costume," what you show to the customer must come from who you are, not who you pretend to be.

Katie never commented on my obvious Southern accent. "You ain't from around here, are you?" would not have exactly made me feel like a neighbor. She was warm and a bit of a character, with a nonstop friendly tease. But even at the summit of her impishness, she never lost sight of the fact that I contributed to the currency that funded her wages. Katie's motivation was clearly not about tit for tat, her honor for my honorarium. She seemed genuinely thrilled and respectful that I was there to eat Don's Fatso Burger.

Animation must always reflect respect. One important dimension of this is the degree to which the animation strategy fits your situation. The customer bond must make sense in its context. A complimentary bottle of champagne at a fast-food drive-through would be as dissonant as a free serving of French fries at a five-star restaurant, but a congruent connection is more than matching connection with conditions, or affirmation with ambiance. The connection must also be congruent with tone and style. As a former service-quality instructor at the Disney Institute put it: "Disney makes magic with pixie dust. Whatever they do smells right, tastes right, sounds right as well as feels right. Bottom line, it is theatrically pure." Animation wows your customers when it is theatrically pure.

Customer connections are about forging strong links, not about making superficial contacts. They create a bond when they stir our emotions, not just get our attention. This means they must be laced with spirit, energy, and attitude. The most notable customer-wowing service providers are masters at balancing the familiar, the comfortable, and the respectful with the sparkly. In a word, animation is their forte.

Just like White's Restaurant, the culture that supports, encourages, and nurtures animation will be the one that attracts and retains devoted customers. Animation is a service strategy that makes you, as well as your customer, smile. Animation stays in the customer's memory banks for a long time afterward, or it quickly surfaces when someone mentions the service provider who created it. And it makes you, the service provider, look forward to delivering it with all the excitement of a nine-year-old waiting for Santa.

2

My company created my role for one reason: to make you very happy, sir. And the best part is, they picked me to do it!

~ Charlie, a doorman at the Marriott Quorum, Dallas Texas

Delighting others requires a kind of mindfulness of the impact of what one does has on the lives of others. It is one of the things that makes life worthwhile. Delighting others is our shot at making a lasting mark in our short passage on this little planet.

~ Steve Denning, *Forbes* June 29, 2011

Check your ATTITUDE ...
Which one are you?

2

Approachable		Angry
Teachable		Testy
Tireless		Tiresome
Inspired	OR	Irritable
Terrifically optimistic		Terribly pessimistic
Upbeat		Upset
Determined		Depressed
Eager to find solutions		Eager to assign blame

2

You can get glad as fast as you can get mad.

~ Daisy Dimples Williams, my grandma

Your attitude, not your aptitude, will determine your altitude.

~ Zig Ziglar, motivational speaker, author

CHOOSE TO BE HAPPY, NO MATTER WHAT

One of my all-time favorite books is *Happiness Is a Choice*, by Barry Neil Kaufman. Barry and his wife had a baby boy, their third child, who was diagnosed as autistic. At first, the couple was devastated; they thought their lives were ruined and their child was doomed to a hopeless future.

Once they worked through their initial reaction to the diagnosis, though, they made a huge decision: They chose to be happy. They said, "We can let this situation drag us into depression and self-pity, or we can decide to love our child, make a nurturing family for him, and have a good life together." They chose the latter.

They rejected the advice of doctors who told them to put the child in an institution and to move on with their lives. Instead, they completely redesigned their home and their lives to meet the needs of their autistic toddler. He couldn't meet them in their world, so they met him in his. They sat on the floor and played with him, mimicking his shrieks, whoops, and hand gestures.

Bit by bit, they were able to build rapport with their son, teach him new behaviors, and coax him further and further into normalcy. The boy grew and thrived under his parents' unconditional love, patience, and teaching. It was a long, challenging process, but he graduated from high school, then college, with honors. And throughout those challenging years, Barry Neil Kaufman and his wife simply chose to be happy.

We cannot control what happens to us in life, but we *can* control the attitude we adopt in response to life's events. Happiness is always available; all we need to do is choose it.

2

Life isn't about waiting for the storm to pass ...
It's about learning to dance in the rain.

~ Vivian Greene, author, entrepreneur

TIPS AND TOOLS:

The human mind is a mismatch detector; it always notices what's wrong before it notices what's right. It's just the way our minds work; this probably served a survival function at some point in our evolutionary history. But just because our minds have a negative default position doesn't mean that you're stuck with a negative, unhappy, fault-finding mind. Neuroscientists are discovering more and more ways in which our minds are malleable and flexible—they call it neuroplasticity. What that means is that you and I can literally retrain our minds! And if you can retrain your mind, that means you can change your attitude—in any situation.

Here are a few tips to jump-start an attitude adjustment when you need one:

1. **Celebrate what's right with the world.** All around you, there are good things happening—kids going to school to learn, people engaged in work activities, plants and trees growing and blossoming, families enjoying time together, pets bringing love and cuddles to our lives, and much, much more. Take five minutes every morning and five minutes every afternoon to look around you, wherever you happen to be, and look for all the good things going. Make a note of those things. Be happy about them. Celebrate them.

2. **Practice active gratitude.** While you're on your way to work, look for three things to be grateful for. Say a quiet thank-you for each of those things. When you're out walking your dog, look for three things to be grateful for. Say, "Thank you," out loud to reinforce your gratitude. While you're at home, take a few minutes to walk around in your living space and notice the things you really love—an old quilt, a beloved book, a favorite chair, the view from one of your windows, a family photo, a memento from a special occasion, and so on—and touch those things. Say, "Thank you," quietly, savoring the warm feelings of

gratitude. In your workplace, look for three people or things that you're grateful for; gaze at them for a minute and let yourself feel the appreciation. Practicing gratitude is the fastest way to snap yourself out of any negative or unhappy feelings.

3. **Catch people doing something right – and acknowledge them for it.** It's always easy to notice when someone is doing something you don't like and to let it make you unhappy. It takes a little more effort and energy to watch for people doing things right—but it is so worth it! You can have a powerful positive influence on your workplace and the people in it if you will make it a habit to notice when others do things right—and say something about it. Giving someone a pat on the back—an attaboy or atta girl is a great way to reinforce that person's positive attitude and your own as well.

PRACTICE THE PLATINUM RULE

3

I've learned that people
will forget what you
said;
people will forget
what you did;
but people will never
forget how you made
them feel.

~ Maya Angelou, poet, professor,
author

THE PLATINUM RULE

Like millions of other people, I was taught the Golden Rule when I was a child. My father told me, "Treat other people the way you'd like to be treated." It made sense to me and seemed like a good idea at the time.

As I grew up, however, I discovered that the Golden Rule often didn't work all that well. I would treat someone the way I liked to be treated, and rather than making them happy, it sometimes made them upset. I didn't know what to make of this.

Over time, I figured it out. The Golden Rule assumes that everyone is like me ... but that's a mistaken assumption! In truth of fact, the older I get and the more people I meet, the more I see how *different* we are from one another. We have cultural differences, age differences, gender differences, political differences, personality differences, sense-of-humor differences, and many, many more—too many to count! One person's trash is another person's treasure. One person's delicious treat may be distasteful to others. Courtesy to one person may give offense to another.

Here's a simple example: Years ago, I had a young Korean college student doing a part-time internship with my business. One day, he made a serious mistake, so I called him into my office to have a conversation about it. The whole time I was talking to him, he never once looked at me. He averted his eyes and kept his gaze fixed on his hands in his lap. The longer we talked, the more annoyed I became. Why? Because in my culture, it is expected that you make eye contact with someone who is talking to you. (My father's words so often come back to me: "Look at me when I'm talking to you!" he would snap when he was scolding me.)

What I didn't know was that in Korean culture, it is *disrespectful* to make eye contact with authority figures—teachers, bosses, parents, and others. By keeping his eyes averted, this young man was showing respect for me, but I thought just the opposite. I thought he was being passive-aggressive by refusing to look at me!

See how easily things can go wrong when we follow the Golden Rule? Because people are so different in so many ways, assuming that others want to be treated like we do can result in serious interpersonal mistakes—especially in terms of customer service.

What's the answer? The Platinum Rule: "Treat others the way *they* want to be treated." How do I find out how they want to be treated? I ask them. To learn someone else's preferences and how they'd like me to interact with them, I need to spend some time talking to them, determining what's important to them, what their buying motives are, what they value in a product or service. In other words, I need to get to know them, to understand them as unique human beings who are similar to me in some ways but very different from me in others. I need to build a relationship with them based on respect, authentic interest in serving them well, and a desire to meet their needs.

You can see how important it is to start with beginner's mind. I mustn't assume that I know who people are and what's important to them. Instead, I must approach each person with no assumption, no preconceived idea, no judgment. Only then can I meet them where they are truly, authentically, compassionately.

You can also see how important attitude is, can't you? If my attitude is arrogant and bored, other people pick up on that and won't want to do business with me. If my attitude is frustrated and stressed, they'll pick up on that, too. And if my attitude is positive and upbeat, others can feel my energy and will enjoy interacting with me.

We start with beginner's mind—no assumptions, no preconceived ideas. We make sure we have a good attitude in dealing with others. And we practice the Platinum Rule—we treat others the way they want to be treated. With these three steps, we are well on our way to fulfilling relationships—with our customers, with our coworkers, with our bosses, and with everyone we meet!

If you will please people, you must please them in
their own way; and as you cannot make them
what they should be, you must take them as they
are.

~ Lord Chesterfield, British statesman

3

Whatever your business is, talk to your customers
and provide them with what they want. It makes
sense.

~ Robert Bowman, CEO Major League Baseball
Advanced Media

What is AUTHENTIC service?

Aware

Understanding

Tactful

Honest

Empathetic

Natural

Tuned In

Interested

Caring

3

Revolve your world around the customer
and more customers will revolve around you.

~ Heather Williams

3

When the customer comes first, the customer will last.

~ Robert Half

DON'T MAKE SALES CALLS, MAKE SERVICE CALLS

Chuck Chamberlain was a successful businessman in Los Angeles. He was in the business of designing and building grocery stores. Recently, I listened to a CD series of lectures he gave many years ago entitled "A New Pair of Glasses."

At one point during his lectures, Chuck explained how he had become wealthy and successful in business. He said he did not make sales calls—he made *service calls*. He was in the business of helping others be successful in their businesses. When Chuck called on a potential customer, he viewed it as an opportunity to be of service.

"How can I help you?" Chuck would ask. "How's your business doing? What's working? What isn't working? Tell me about the problems you're struggling with." He would listen with no agenda. He would listen with an open mind and an open heart, with a genuine desire to help the other guy build his business.

If Chuck could help the other guy, he would. If he couldn't offer anything to help, he would try to think if he knew anyone else who could, and he'd refer the customer to that other person.

Chuck went on to explain that on two or three occasions, he went to call on potential customers with a different motivation—he was broke and desperately needed to make a sale. "Whenever I felt like that—*I need this sale; I* have *to make some money today*—I came away empty-handed. I never made a sale that way."

In other words, when Chuck called on people to *get* something from them, he failed. When he called on people to serve them, he always got the sale.

People are smart and intuitive. They can pick up on your energy, and they know when you're trying to get something from them. They often resist, because they know the conversation is all about you, but they also know when your intent is to help, to be of service, to contribute, to help them achieve their goals. When you approach them with that intent, they welcome you with open arms.

Important Words for
SERVING RIGHT*

The 10 important words to say:
I apologize for our mistake. Let me make it right.

The 9 important words to say:
Thank you for your business. Please come back again.

The 8 important words to say:
I'm not sure, but I will find out.

The 7 important word to say:
What else can I do for you?

The 6 important words to say:
What is most convenient for you?

The 5 important words to say:
How may I serve you?

The 4 important words to say:
How did we do?

The 3 important words to say:
Glad you're here!

The 2 important words to say:
Thank you.

The 1 important word to say:
Yes.

* from "Serve Right" by Steve Ventura

TIPS AND TOOLS:

How do you exchange the Golden Rule for the Platinum Rule? Here are a few simple tips for practicing this new way of relating to others.

1. **Appearances can be deceiving so don't judge a book by its cover.** Avoid the tendency to make assumptions about someone based on their appearance – including age, gender, race, attire, and grooming.

2. **Ask good questions.** You don't want to ask yes-or-no questions; you want to ask high-value open-ended questions that will yield meaningful information about who the other person is and how that person wants to be treated

3. **Be aware of your nonverbal communication as well as your verbal interaction with another person.** Your body language, facial expression, posture, and tone of voice all make a powerful impression on others, for good or for bad. Make sure your facial expression is welcoming, your smile warm and inviting. You want to put the other person at ease, build trust, and let the person know you're sincerely interested in serving him or her.

4. **If you mis-step somehow and inadvertently offend someone, apologize quickly and let the person know your intention was good.** Even if that person doesn't say anything, you can often tell you've made a mistake by the facial expression or body language of the person you're interacting with. Don't just pretend nothing's wrong; ask for feedback and be sincere in your desire to get things back on track and make everything right.

Remember: *Who you're being* **speaks louder than what you're saying.**

GREAT SERVICE BEGINS AT HOME

If you're not serving a customer, your job is to be serving someone who is.

~ Jan Carlson, president SAS airlines

4

Remember Your *Internal* Customers

by Steve Ventura

Several weeks ago, I was talking to a friend of mine. He asked what I was working on. I told him I was writing a book about customer service. His response: "That's nice. Too bad it's not a book that applies to me; otherwise, I'd want to get a copy." I asked why he thought customer service wasn't relevant for him. His answer revealed just how misinformed he was: "Because I don't deal with customers. I keep our computers running ... I've got an 'inside' job."

Sound familiar? Do you know someone like that? Do you have a friend who thinks that customer service applies only to front-line employees dealing directly with patrons who walk in your door or call on the phone? If so, your friend is as misinformed as mine. Both of them need to get their heads straight!

The fact is, everyone with a job provides some kind of service to other people. It doesn't matter if you stock shelves, run a website, manufacture parts, issue paychecks, or clean toilets— you're doing it for someone else.

That someone may be your boss, a fellow team member, or perhaps a person in another department or location in your organization. And because they are the individuals you do things for, they share the same label with everyone from the *outside* who does business with you. They are *customers*. They are *your* customers ... your *internal* customers. And as such, they deserve the very same courtesies, attention, effort, and quality work that external customers should receive. Why wouldn't they?

So, tell your friend to remember this: When it comes to the world of the employed, one way or another ...

everyone is in the customer service business!

Internal customer service is the service provided to colleagues and other departments within an organization, as well as vendors and anyone else an employee interacts with to get their job done. When a colleague asks you for information regarding a project or when an employee calls Human Resources for information regarding their vacation time—that is internal customer service. How you or any other member of the company responds to such requests is reflective of how your customer's issues are handled. If you want to provide world-class customer service ... you will need to start with providing great internal customer service to your employees.

~ Rachel Miller, consultant

4

Good leaders must first become good servants.

~ Robert Greenleaf, *Servant Leadership*

How may I SERVE you? By being ...

Sincerely interested in who you are,

Eager to meet your needs,

Responsive and respectful,

Very committed to resolving any problems, and

Empathetic and generous.

4

There is a domino effect between internal customer satisfaction and external customer satisfaction. In order to produce happy external customers (the ones who buy your product/service), it is important and imperative to build customer satisfaction between the internal customers.

~ Teri Yanovitch, customer service consultant

We see our customers as invited guests to a party, and we are the hosts. It's our job every day to make every important aspect of the customer experience a little bit better.

~ Jeff Bezos, founder and CEO of Amazon.com

4

TIPS AND TOOLS:

How can you ensure that your internal customer service is top-notch?

Start with these six simple steps.

1. **Identify who your internal customers are.** If you're the bookkeeper, who do you serve? If you're the stock boy, whom do you serve? If you're a secretary, whom do you serve? If you're someone's assistant, it's clear that you serve that person, but do you serve other employees as well? No matter what your job title, you are undoubtedly providing service to some-one else within the business—probably several some-ones. Make a list of the coworkers and/or bosses you serve.

2. **Talk to your internal customers to ask specifi-cally what each needs from you to do his or her own job well.** What are your customers' expectations of you? How do they need you to serve them so they can serve others?

3. **Ask your internal customers what you currently do that disappoints or gets in the way of them doing a great job.** In other words, ask for their com-plaints and concerns. Remember: Feedback is the breakfast of champions. You can't improve your ser-vice if you don't know how you're doing now.

4. **Ask your internal customers what you could do to make their jobs easier and more productive.** What suggestions and/or requests do they have for you? What do they need you to do more of?

5. **Document what you learn from your internal customers.** Take notes of what they tell you; don't trust your memory to remember everything. Taking notes lets your internal customers know that you're listening to them and taking their feedback seriously. Then schedule regular follow-up meetings to see how things are going in terms of improving your service to them.

6. Keep your supervisors and managers informed about what you're doing to improve your internal customer service and, thereby, external customer service.

4

A COMPLAINT IS A GIFT

5

Your most unhappy customers are your greatest source of learning.

~ Bill Gates, founder of Microsoft

A COMPLAINT IS A GIFT

by BJ Gallagher

5

"What a concept!" I marveled to myself as I read Janelle Barlow's book, *A Complaint is a Gift*. It's a business book about customer service and the importance of getting feedback, especially negative feedback, from customers. Barlow and her coauthor, Claus Møller, assert that complaints are not problems to be avoided but actually gifts to be welcomed. What a radical way to think about negative feedback!

Complaints are important for several reasons, Barlow writes:

- You don't know how to improve your product or service if you don't know what's wrong.
- Customer complaints can give you ideas for new products and services.
- Complaints give you valuable information about what's important to people, what they're willing to spend money on.

Complaints also tell you that the customer still wants to do business with you—she still cares about the relationship she has with your company and she wants you to fix the problem so she can continue to do business with you. Most customers don't complain; they just take their business elsewhere because they've given up hope of getting what they need from you.

The problem is, most people think that customer complaints are bad. They mistakenly think that no complaints means no problems. But as long as you're in business, you will always have problems—it's part and parcel of doing business. The important thing to focus on is how you handle those problems when they occur.

That's why a complaint is really a gift. Just as we thank someone who gives us a birthday gift, we should thank someone
who brings us a complaint. This person has given something
valuable, something useful, something that can help make our
business stronger and more profitable, and we should treat the
complaint as the gift that it really is.

This is a great concept! I kept thinking as I read her book. *And
what's more, it applies not only to business but also to personal
relationships!* I thought about all the different ways that complaints come into our lives: our parents complain about some
aspect of our behavior; our lovers complain when they feel
neglected; our friends complain if we have a misunderstand-
ing; our neighbors complain about a problem with our home;
our children complain if they need something from us that we
haven't provided. Complaints are simply a normal part of what
it means to live in relationships with other people.

After reading Barlow's book, I started reacting differently
when someone in my life complained to me. I learned to make
the interaction a learning experience rather than a battle. I
saw how to use the complaint to make our relationship better
rather than letting the complaint tear us apart. If someone in
my life has a complaint about my business (or me), I can be
reassured by the fact that the person is at least still talking to
me. This tells me that the person still cares about our relationship and wants me to make a change so we can continue to
work together. If the person stops talking to me, that's when I
should worry—that's when the person has given up and taken
his business elsewhere.

In treating complaints as gifts, Barlow teaches a step-by-step
process:

1. Thank the person for his complaint. Tell him how
    much you appreciate his taking the time to tell you
    about his problem.

2. Tell him why you're thanking him: because you care
    about your relationship, and his complaint gives you
    an opportunity to address anything that isn't working
    for him.

3. Apologize for the fact that he is unhappy. Note: You don't assume guilt or say that it is your fault; you simply say, "I'm sorry you're having this problem."

4. Promise to do whatever you can to help solve the problem.

5. Ask for more information or clarification or specifics so you can fully understand the source of his unhappiness.

6. Take whatever steps you can to correct the problem—focusing on things that are within your control. If it's something out of your control, explain that. If it is something that really has nothing to do with you at all, this is the point in the discussion when you are most likely to discover that.

7. Ask if he feels his complaint is being addressed. If not, go back to the beginning of the process.

8. Make sure to learn from the situation. Complaints can provide ideas for new products or services, as well as tell you about weak links in your organization.

Most important of all, always emphasize what you can do, rather than what you *can't*. Look for what is possible, rather than telling him what is impossible. Pointing out what you *can't do* simply makes you both more frustrated.

This complaint-is-a-gift notion is not one that comes naturally to anyone. None of us likes to hear negative feedback. But feedback is the breakfast of champions. If we can hear what's behind the complaint—the desire to fix something that's bothering the other person—we can see how the complaint really *is* a gift!

Customers don't expect you to be perfect.
They do expect you to fix things when they go
wrong.

> ~ Donald Porter, VP, British Airways

A customer is the most important person ever in
this company. ...
A customer is not dependent on us; we are dependent on him.
A customer is not an interruption of our work, he
is the purpose of it.
We are not doing a favor by serving him,
he is doing us a favor by giving us the opportunity to do so.

> ~Leon Leonwood (L.L.) Bean

What Makes for Good COMMUNICATION?

5

Clear, simple words

Open minds

Mutual commitment to understand

Mutual commitment to be understood

Unambiguous meaning

Nonjudgmental words and tone

Integrity of intention

Congruence of verbal message and body language

Articulate, authentic expression

Timely, appropriate feedback

Intent to listen and learn

Ongoing clarification and re-clarification

Non-defensive attitude

Statistics suggest that when customers complain, business owners and managers ought to get excited about it. The complaining customer represents a huge opportunity for more business.

~ Zig Ziglar, motivation speaker, author

I VOTE WITH MY WALLET

by Steve Ventura

5

There was a day, not that long ago, when I hit the trifecta of poor customer service. I remember it far too well. It all happened when I went to a local restaurant for lunch. Driving through the lot, in an effort to avoid parking in the "boonies," I noticed one vacant spot right in front of the restaurant entrance. I sped up to take advantage of this good fortune, but alas, another car pulled into the slot as I was approaching. Although slightly ticked at first, I realized, "Hey, some other guy merely beat me to it." And I quickly became okay with what had occurred—okay, that is, until the other guy exited his car and I saw that he was wearing a uniform for this restaurant. Now I was *really* ticked! I don't care if he wanted a good parking spot; so did I. After all, I was the customer. I considered taking my business elsewhere, but I didn't. I parked way in the back and went in for lunch.

There was a line of people waiting for tables. I got in the back of it and slowly worked my way forward. Finally, I made it to the front of the line. Just as the girl behind the register desk was about to address me, two on-duty employees came up to her and asked for their paychecks. The girl looked at me, said, "I'll be with you shortly," and began a three-minute search for the employee checks—while I, the customer, was left waiting.

Finally, I got my table, made my order, ate my lunch, and was ready for my tab so I could pay up and leave. My waiter, however, was nowhere in sight. I sat semi-patiently for several minutes and then got up and walked across the room, looking for someone to help me. I spotted another waiter and asked if he could get my bill. His response: "I'm sorry, I just started my break. I'm sure your waiter will be back shortly." With that, he walked away. Eventually, I got and paid my bill—and I walked away, too. I haven't been back since then.

One day, one place, three examples of employees putting their own needs and wants before those of a customer. Maybe they didn't think about what they were doing. Maybe they just didn't care. Either way, there will be one *less* patron contributing to their future income.

Here's the deal: When I choose to do business with a business, it don't expect its employees to act like I am royalty and they are medieval peasants. I do, however, expect them to make me feel special and important; I expect them to act like they understand (and appreciate) that I am the one who *really* pays their salaries … that I am the reason that their business exists. Show me that courtesy, and you have a customer for life. Fail to do so, and I'm history.

As a customer, have you had experiences similar to the ones I described? Did they make you as mad as they did me? If so, remember them … learn from them … make sure you don't do the same things to the people *you're* there to serve.

There is only one boss: the customer. And he can fire everybody in the company from the chairman on down, simply by spending his money some-where else.

~ Sam Walton, founder of Walmart

It is not the employer who pays the wages. Employers only handle the money. It is the customer who pays the wages.

~ Henry Ford, founder of the Ford Motor Company

FEEDBACK IS THE BREAKFAST OF CHAMPTIONS

5

The best car salesman I ever met made his money selling to repeat customers and the many friends they referred to him. I asked him to tell me the secret to his success.

"It's not a secret," he said. "Anybody can do it. Whenever I sell a car, before the customer leaves the dealership, I ask him to do me a favor: 'If you liked my service, tell all your friends. And if you didn't like my service, tell *me*. Tell me now, because if you're unhappy with any aspect of this deal—anything at all—I want to fix it. I want the opportunity to make things right with you before you leave.'"

"In other words, you ask your customer to help you improve the quality of the car-buying experience," I replied, "*and* you ask your customer to advertise you and your great service."

"Yup," he said and nodded. "Because an unhappy customer will tell dozens of his friends, but happy customers usually only tell a couple of friends. So I want to encourage my happy customers to tell *more* people ... *and* I want any unhappy to tell *me*, so I can turn him into a happy customer."

"That's really smart," I told him. "Customer-service research indicates that if you resolve a customer's complaint, he will be *more* loyal than a customer who had no complaint at all!"

"Well, I don't know about research or anything," he said. "All I know is if my customer is unhappy, I don't want him telling all his friends—I want him to tell *me*. His friends can't fix his problem—but I *can*—and I will. That's why I've got so much repeat and referral business. I never have to go out looking for brand-new customers. ... Customers come to me instead because they know they'll get great service. I outsell every other salesperson who works here because of that."

I share that car salesman's "secret" everywhere I go. **"If you liked my service, tell all your friends. If you didn't like my service, tell *me* so I can fix it and make things right by you."**

He truly understands that feedback is the breakfast of champions … and that a complaint is a gift.

Those who enter to buy support me.
Those who come to flatter please me.
Those who complain teach me how I may
please others so that more will come.
Only those hurt me who are displeased
but do not complain.

~ Marshall Field, department store founder and CEO

TIPS AND TOOLS:

Does everyone in your business understand that a complaint is a gift? Do they understand that feedback is the breakfast of champions and that all feedback—positive and negative—is helpful? Do you know how complaint-friendly your business is?

Here are five keys for making sure that you're getting the feedback you need from customers:

1. **Your business' complaint philosophy.** All employees should understand the value in getting feedback from customers. Make it easy for customers to bring problems to your attention. Customers feel appreciated when they give you their feedback—good, bad, or indifferent.

2. **Employees know how to respond effectively to complaints.** Everyone is trained in how to treat complaints as gifts. Frontline employees are empowered to fix problems quickly and effectively.

3. **Internal complaints are handled as gifts, too.** As we discussed in a previous chapter, good customer service begins at home. Employee complaints are welcomed—even encouraged—to continuously improve the effectiveness and success of your business.

4. **Policies and procedures are practical and sensible, as well as flexible.** Rigid policies, bureaucratic red tape, and too much procedural hassle will hurt your employees' ability to resolve customer-service problems. Keep policies to a minimum, and frequently reevaluate them to make sure they're not getting in the way of service effectiveness.

5. **Management practices set the tone for employees.** Business success starts at the top. Owners, managers, and supervisors must welcome complaints, encourage feedback from customers and employees, and walk their customer-service talk in every aspect of the business.

CREATE A CUSTOMER-CENTRIC BUSINESS

6

In the long run, no matter how good or successful you are or how clever or crafty, your business and its future are in the hands of the people you hire.

~ Akio Morita, co-founder, Sony

PEOPLE REALLY *ARE*
YOUR GREATEST RESOURCE!

I can't tell you how many businesses I've worked with who assert, "Our people are our greatest asset," but when I look at their people practices—hiring procedures, training programs, compensation practices, incentive and reward systems, and management practices—I discover that they don't really mean it. It's a nice slogan, but many businesses, small and large, don't walk their talk. As we say where I come from in Texas, these folks are "all hat and no cattle."

MISTAKE #1: Hiring the wrong people. Some business owners have what I call the "third-eye hiring test": If you don't have a third eye, you're hired! You laugh, but I'm serious. Too many entrepreneurs don't have a clue what to look for when screening and hiring people. They make hiring decisions based on "a gut feeling." They hire people they like, rather than people who have the best skills, talents, and abilities for the job. They hire friends or family members, counting on personal loyalty and friendship to get the job done.

HIRE RIGHT: Invest time and energy in screening and hiring the right people for the job.

MISTAKE #2: Failing to consider an applicant's *potential,* as well as their experience. If you are willing to hire only people whose past experience is the same job you're hiring them to do now, you're looking only at the past and not at the future, and you're very likely to get someone who will be bored within a very short time, because there's no challenge in doing the same job again and again. You want to look at an applicant's potential as well as experience. You want to put more emphasis on the person's ability to grow, learn, stretch, and take on bigger, tougher challenges and more responsibility in the coming years. An employee who continues to grow and learn is a happy, productive employee. Don't look just at what someone *has done*; also look at what he or she *can do*!

HIRE RIGHT: Look at each person's generic skills – their toolkit of skills that can be applied to a variety of jobs. (For instance: verbal communication skills, financial skills, problem-solving abilities, organizing skills, project management skills, ability to work under pressure, ability to prioritize tasks, ability to handle angry customers, history of rebounding from mistakes, and so on.)

MISTAKE #3: Looking for hired hands instead of hired heads. If you hire only people who are good at taking orders and following instructions, you are significantly limiting the future growth of your business. After all, those folks on the front line, those who are closest to the customer, are those in the best position to hear what customers need and want. That means they're also in a great position to come up with good ideas about new products and services. You want to hire smart people who can think, innovate, and create. You also want them to solve problems quickly and effectively. You want them to be flexible and resourceful in handling day-to-day things that come up in any business.

HIRE RIGHT: Give applicants appropriate job-skills tests to determine their ability to solve problems, be resourceful, and think beyond the obvious.

MISTAKE #4: Failing to train people. I am often amazed at how many business owners throw people into jobs without adequate training. They figure, "Well, anybody can answer the phone because everybody knows how to do that already," or, "How much training does somebody need to wait tables? It's a no-brainer." Worse yet, some think, "If I have to train them, then I shouldn't hire them. I want people who are already trained." What these bosses don't realize is that employees require regular instruction, feedback, and coaching. People are not machines—you don't just plug them in someplace and then ignore or neglect them. If you want people to perform well in their jobs, you must make sure they are thoroughly trained in all aspects of the job. Don't assume anything. Invest in good training, and you'll reap the rewards for years to come.

TRAIN RIGHT: If you hire the right people for the job, half your training job is already done, but you still have to do the other half! Make sure that all new hires are thoroughly trained before you have them interact with customers. Consider having a buddy system, a sort of apprenticeship, in which more senior employees do the training, coaching, and bringing of new hires up to speed.

MISTAKE #5: Failing to reward good performance. It is a truism that you get what you pay for. When employees feel that they're paid a fair wage for a good day's work, they feel valued, respected, and motivated to do a good job. If they feel underpaid, they feel underappreciated and undervalued, which affects their motivation and commitment to the job. Money isn't everything, of course. Employees are also motivated by intangible things such as praise, recognition, attention, encouragement, and appreciation. If the people in your business aren't performing at the level you'd like them to, one of the first places to look for the reason is in the mirror: What are *you* doing to acknowledge and appreciate them? Does the paycheck you give them indicate how much you value their contribution to the business? People do what they get rewarded for.

REWARD RIGHT: Feedback is the breakfast of champions! Make sure you show your appreciation for a job well done, in both financial and nonfinancial ways.

6

We decided that we wanted to build our brand to be about the very best customer service and the very best customer experience. We believe that customer service shouldn't be just a department, it should be the entire company.

~ Tony Hsieh, founder and CEO of Zappos.com

The goal as a company is to have customer service that is not just the best, but legendary.

~ Sam Walton, founder of Walmart

Do what you do so well that they will want to see it again and bring their friends.

~ Walt Disney, founder of Disneyland

What Qualities Make a Good LEADER?

Listening and learning

Embracing others' diverse skills, abilities, and styles

Articulate, authentic expression

Driven by good values and ethics

Eager to make a positive difference

Ready and able to adapt as marketplace changes

6

Four Principles for Running a Business in Good Times and Bad

by Leslie Yerkes and Charles Decker

In this age of headlines about corporate executives run amok, Jack and Dianne Hartman, the owners of the El Espresso, are the kind of businesspeople who deserve a little good press. For more than thirty years, they have stayed true to their values and their principles. In the process, they have created a business that has earned the reputation for serving Seattle's best coffee—coffee good enough to make people willing to line up in the rain to buy a cup!

Applying simple principles consistently has created a place where everyone wants to be a regular, where the customer is known and respected, and where there is a clear connection between serving people and running a business.

The secret to the long-term success at the El Espresso is a recipe for life as well as for work—we call it the four Ps: PASSION, PEOPLE, PERSONAL, and PRODUCT. Pour some of each into your work and your professional relationships to experience satisfaction and success in all that you do.

It's all about PASSION.

- Do what you love, and you won't work another day in your life.

- Listen to your heart and discover your personal source for positive energy.

- Build your work around your passion.

- Pursue a vision—blend your work and play.

- Share it generously with others.

- Create a climate in which everybody can freely express his or her own passion.

- It's about what you're doing being a natural extension of yourself.

Make it happen with PEOPLE.

- Look for people who share your values.

- Abandon the use of fear and force in relationships.

- Communicate clearly and develop shared expectations .

- Honor and uplift all the individuals you deal with, and recognize their contributions.

- Bring the best of your whole self to work each day.

- Assume the positive—trust yourself and extend that trust to others.

- Help others to succeed.

- Have few rules and no secrets.

- Create the stage for every employee to receive a standing ovation daily.

You've got to make it PERSONAL.

- Practice simple gestures of courtesy.

- Be authentic and well-intentioned in all situations.

- Initiate positive interactions.

- Open the door and go beyond the transaction—be generous.

- Act like an owner and host.

- Make it an experience—treat everyone as unique and valued.

- It's about engaging and not just your hands but your head and your heart in your work.

PRODUCT is the foundation.

- Be as passionate about your product as you are about the people.

- Find little ways to differentiate and delight.

- Listen to the customer.

- Treat every interaction as the first and best.

- Create confidence with consistency.

- Earn a reputation for having a product that your customers cannot stop talking about.

Create a service culture with these behaviors, and you'll find yourself contributing to a workplace that is so positively contagious that it will be hard to decide who is happier—the employees or the customers.

6

Customers don't always know what they want.
The decline in coffee-drinking was due to the fact
that most of the coffee people bought was stale
and they weren't enjoying it. Once they tasted
ours and experienced what we call "the third
place"—a gathering place between home and
work where they were treated with respect—they
found we were filling a need they didn't know
they had.

~ Howard Schultz, chairman and CEO, Starbucks

TIPS AND TOOLS:

How do you make sure that *your* business is customer-centric? Here are a few ideas to help keep everyone focused.

1. **Visit businesses that are well-known for their superb customer service.** Disneyland and Disneyworld, Nordstrom department store, Southwest Airlines, Zappos shoes, Amazon, Federal Express, Mrs. Fields are great examples, among others. If you can't visit them personally, read books about them or read case studies from the Harvard Business School. Study the best of the best; adopt and adapt their customer-service practices into your own business.

2. **Think about your own happy experiences of being a customer at a place of business in your community.** What made you want to go back to that place? What did the employees do that made you feel wonderful? What can you learn from them to incorporate into your own business?

3. **Think about any *unhappy* experiences you've had as a customer.** What mistakes did those businesses make? We can often learn powerful lessons about what not to do by reflecting on other businesses' mistakes and failures.

AIM FOR CUSTOMER *DELIGHT* ... NOT JUST SATISFACTION

Being on par in terms of price and quality only gets you into the game. Service wins the game.

~ Tony Allesandra, customer-service expert

JOHNNY THE BAGGER

by Barbara Glanz

A few years ago, I was hired by a large supermarket chain to lead a customer-service program, to build customer loyalty. During my speech, I said, "Every one of you can make a difference and create memories for your customers that will motivate them to come back." How?

Put your personal signature on the job. Think about something you can do for your customers to make them feel special—memories that will make them come back.

About a month after I had spoken, I received a phone call from a nineteen-year-old bagger named Johnny. He proudly informed me he was a Down syndrome individual and told me his story.

"I liked what you talked about," he said, "but at first I didn't think I could do anything special for our customers. After all, I'm just a bagger. Then I had an Idea," Johnny said.

"Every night after work, I'd come home and find a thought for the day. If I can't find a saying I like," he added, "I'd just think one up."

When Johnny had a good thought for the day, his dad helped him set it up on the computer and print multiple copies. Johnny cut out each quote and signed the back. Then he'd bring the quotes to work the next day.

"When I finish bagging someone's groceries, I put my thought for the day in their bag and say, 'Thanks for shopping with us.'"

It touched me to think that this young man—with a job most people would say is not important—had made it important by creating precious memories for all of his customers.

A month later, the store manager called me. "You won't believe what happened. When I was making my rounds today, I found Johnny's checkout line was three times longer than anyone else's. It went all the way down the frozen food aisle, so I quickly announced, 'We need more cashiers; get more lanes open,' as I tried to get people to change lanes. But no one would move. They said, 'No that's OK. We want to be in Johnny's lane. We want his thought for the day.'"

The store manager continued, "It was a joy to watch Johnny delight the customers. I got a lump in my throat when one woman said, 'I used to shop at your store once a week, but now I come by every time I go by, because I want to get Johnny's thought for the day.'"

A few months later, the manager called me again. "Johnny has transformed our store. Now when the floral department has a broken flower or unused corsage, they find an elderly women or a little girl and pin it on them. Everyone has had a lot of fun creating memories. Our customers are talking about us. ... They're coming back and bringing their friends."

A wonderful spirit of service spread throughout the entire store ... all because Johnny chose to make a difference.

Johnny's idea wasn't nearly as innovative as it was loving. It came from his heart. It was real. That's what touched the customers, his peers ... and those who read this story.

We wildly underestimate the power of the tiniest personal touch.

~ Tom Peters, *In Search of Excellence*

Giving people a little more than they expect
is a good way to get back a lot more than you
would expect.

~ Robert Half, CEO of the world's largest staffing services firm

7

Don't just try to satisfy your customers—satisfaction is not enough. Loyalty is what you need. Think about the word "satisfactory"—what does it mean? It means "okay" or "average." If you are a restaurant owner, would it please you to know that the diners rated your food as "satisfactory"? Wouldn't you rather have them raving that their meals were "amazing" or "fantastic," planning to return again, and telling their friends the same? That's more than satisfaction. That's customer loyalty.

~ Shep Hyken, consultant and author
(from MyCustomer, July 13, 2012)

How to Extend a HELPING HAND ...

Hearing what's needed

Eager to contribute

Listening with compassion

Paying attention to the little things

Intuitively understanding what's helpful and what's not

Never overstepping healthy boundaries

Going out of your way for others

Honoring others' wishes

Asking "What can I do to help?"

Never assuming that you know what's best

Desiring to serve and contribute to others' well-being

Be everywhere, do everything, and never fail to astonish the customer.

~ Macy's motto

7

No one ever attains very eminent success by simply doing what is required; it is the amount and excellence of what is over and above the required that determines the greatness of ultimate distinction.

~ Charles Francis Adams, lawyer, politician, diplomat, writer

EXCEEDING EXPECTATIONS

Marketing consultant and best-selling author Roy H. Williams says that "the first step in exceeding your customer's expectations is to know those expectations."

If you own a self-serve gas station, your customers expect to pump their own gas and wash their own windshields.

If you sell cosmetics, your customers expect a quality product that will enhance a woman's beauty and boost her self-confidence.

If you're in the fine-dining business, your customers expect high-quality food presented attractively, served in a professional manner, at a price commensurate with the dining experience, in surroundings of wonderful ambiance.

How would you *exceed* your customers' expectations?

If you own a gas station, pumping the gas for your customers would certainly surprise them and exceed their expectations!

If you're in the cosmetics business, doing something extra, such as providing free samples with purchase, or providing free facials, would certainly delight the women you serve.

If fine dining is the name of the game you play, exceeding expectations might mean live dinner music, signature cocktails, unique desserts, or something distinctive and exceptional that will surprise and delight your patrons.

In short, the number-one way to make a great impression and to keep customers coming back is with your unique brand of *service*. Gasoline is gasoline, lipstick is lipstick, and a meal is a meal, but what will make *you* stand out from the crowd is the personal brand of service you provide with your product.

I have argued for customer delight, rather than customer satisfaction, because in [today's] strenuous competitive conditions ... most of the winnings in terms of higher margins go to those firms that delight their customers. Thus Apple has 4% of the mobile phone market but 50% of the winnings. If you want the kind of exponential financial success that Apple is enjoying, the customer satisfaction won't hack it. To maintain high margins and thrive, you will need customer excitement and delight.

~ Steve Denning, *Forbes*, June 29, 2011

TIPS AND TOOLS:

Customers' expectations are always changing, influenced by their previous experiences with your business as well as their experiences with other businesses. When someone has a fabulous service experience somewhere else, it raises the bar for you—it means that person's expectations have risen and if you don't rise to the occasion, you just might lose that customer.

Here are a few tips for delighting the folks whom you and your business serve.

1. **Make sure you know what your customers' expectations are.** Don't assume you know what they want and need. Talk to them. Ask them what they like best about doing business with you. Ask them what they don't like, too! Let them know that you value their input—the good, the bad, and even the downright ugly.

2. **Talking with customers gives you ideas for new products and services.** It may give you ideas for reaching new customers with your existing products and services, as well. That's how you grow your business: new products or services for existing customers and new customers for existing products or services. Your customers are a valuable source of innovation if you keep them engaged with in ongoing interaction.

3. **Your competitors can be valuable teachers.** Pay attention to them. Be aware of trends in your industry. Pay special attention to both the leaders and the losers. If you can learn from others' experiences, you'll be that much ahead of the game. You don't have to reinvent the wheel. Be a good student and pay attention to what's happening in the world around you; not just business trends but also social, political, and economic trends affect your business.

CONCLUSION

MAKING A DIFFERENCE ...
ONE CUSTOMER AT A TIME

An old man had a habit of early morning walks on the beach.

One day, after a storm, he saw a human figure in the distance moving like a dancer.

As he came closer, he saw that it was a little girl and she was not dancing but was reaching down to the sand, picking up starfish and very gently throwing them into the ocean.

"Young lady," he asked, "why are you throwing starfish into the ocean?"

"The sun is up, and the tide is going out, and if I do not throw them in, they will die," she answered.

"But young lady," the old man said, "do you not realize that there are miles and miles of beach and starfish all along it? You cannot possibly make a difference."

The little girl listened politely, paused, and then bent down to pick up another starfish, which she threw into the sea. Looking up at the old man, she said, "Well, I made a difference to that one."

How will *you* make
a difference today?

ABOUT
THE AUTHOR

Pam Benson is a true entrepreneur and visionary.

She has conceptualized, launched and operated several successful businesses in the hospitality, construction, and real estate industries. Growing up in Texas, she learned the value of hard work, persistence, and determination. Having weathered our country's many economic recessions and booms, she understands the key to financial success during an uncertain economy.

In addition to being a highly successful restaurateur, Pam is a much-in-demand business coach. She helps entrepreneurs overcome their challenges and obstacles to achieve their maximum potential. She offers solutions for the development of sound business plans and marketing strategies, resulting in increased sales and profitability. Her unique approach unlocks each business owner's unique qualities, skills, and talents, enabling each to reach new levels of business success and personal happiness.

To learn more about Pam Benson and her coaching services, visit www.PamBenson.com

CPSIA information can be obtained at www.ICGtesting.com
Printed in the USA
LVOW02s0538190414

382363LV00004BA/5/P

9 781457 526534